THE HUNTER

-PORTUGAL -

BRAD BAGWELL

Paperback: 978-1-972628-04-1
Ebook: 978-1-972628-05-8

Introduction

This book is another in the series of The Hunter. The Hunter is Justin Hunter, an agent with a secret organization. He, along with Janine, his handler from the organization, and John, another agent who has a group of agents who always seem to be there to help with each mission.

When Justin, Janine and John get together, you know something interesting is going to happen. Once again, the author takes them places where he's traveled, giving the reader a chance to experience different places around the world.

So, sit back and enjoy the latest adventure of The Hunter, as he takes on a mission in Portugal.

Table of Contents

Chapter 1

It's been nearly two weeks in Hawaii, enjoying all the island of Oahu has to offer. Today, Janine and I are at Kualoa Ranch, having fun on their zip lines. Most places have one or two zip lines. Kualoa Ranch has 7 lines. We were just finishing up on number 5 when our phones went off at the same time. That's never a good thing when you're trying to get in some R&R and still have a couple days left. But that's the nature of the game when you're in the business we're in. At least we had most of the past two weeks to get to know each other better.

We read our text message as we were waiting on the platform for the rest of the group to make their way down the line. It seems the daughter of a prominent American businessman had been kidnapped in Portugal and the CIA didn't want to get involved, at least not officially. So, they've asked my organization to try to get the young lady back. Since the only way to get back to our starting point is to take the last two zip lines, and another 20 minutes or so won't make that much difference, we ended up finishing our adventure. The last line has a barrel at about the half- way point that you can try to toss a rock into. If you make it in the barrel as you're going down the zip line, you get a special prize. That wasn't much of a challenge for Janine and me. Unfortunately, it added another 10 minutes to our time there as we gathered our prizes.

On our drive back to Ko Olina to gather our stuff and get cleaned up, Janine arranged for our transportation to Portugal. While the US government didn't want to be overtly involved in the operation to get the hostage back, they were willing to provide military jets to get us there as quickly as possible. As soon as we got back to the Marriott Beach Club in

Ko Olina, we showered and packed in about 15 minutes. We headed to Ford Island in Pearl Harbor and met up with our transport team. That transportation consisted of a couple jet fighters that were capable of nearly Mach 3.

We'd have to slow down a little bit on the way to be refueled by some KC-135's out of Grissom ARB a couple of times, but they would get us to Portugal in about half the time it would take if we tried to get commercial flights.

Since there were no US bases in Portugal, we ended up at a base in France which shared its runway with commercial flights. Unfortunately, there wasn't any room in the fighter jets for any luggage, but, as always, the organization came through for us. When we got to the airport in France, we each had a bag with everything we'd need. From there, it was a short hop to the airport in Porto, Portugal. Coming in on a commercial flight made us less conspicuous.

We quickly got a car and made our way to Braga, which was only about a 30-minute drive. Even though we made the trip from Hawaii to Portugal traveling at nearly Mach 3 the whole way, we were still exhausted. It was hard to rest in a jet fighter. They weren't made for comfort and the G-Suits we had to wear were definitely not conducive to sleeping. Since it was late afternoon, we decided to head to our hotel, check in, then get some dinner. The Villa Garden Braga was a quaint hotel that wasn't too far from several restaurants.

As we got to the lobby and were checking in, John came around the corner to greet us. It was always good to see him since I knew when he was around, all the help I would need would only be a few minutes away.

Janine and I went to our rooms and took quick showers. When we met John back in the lobby, we decided to go to Esperanca Verde for dinner. It was about a 15 – 20-minute walk, which would be good for getting the blood flowing and we needed the exercise. The air was cool and there was a nice breeze, so it was very refreshing. We got a table in the corner, so I could sit with my back to the wall and face the doors. My usual seating arrangement was a hard habit to break. It had kept me safe, so I guess there was no reason to change now.

After we ordered our dinner, John told us about the situation with the young lady, Karen, who had been kidnapped. A few minutes into the briefing, my spidey sense went off. I looked to the front door and saw a familiar face. It was Joseph, one of John's guys who had helped us out in Germany a few weeks ago. It was good to see him. He made his way to our table and dropped off a package. Even though we asked him to stay and have a drink with us, he said he had to get back to the staging area being set up for our operation, since he was the one in charge of getting that done. I could tell he didn't want to disappoint John, Janine or me. I was glad to see he was being given more responsibilities.

The rest of the evening was spent eating dinner and reviewing all the information we had so far. We made our way back to the Villa Garden Braga Hotel at about 10:00 PM. It had been an extremely long day for Janine and me. For John, it had been a normal day. He had spent the last two weeks in Nice, France, so it only took him a couple hours to get to Braga. There were disadvantages to going to Hawaii, but the advantages more than outweighed them, especially since I got to know Janine a lot better. Now to get some rest and get ready to start our operation in the morning.

Chapter 2

Our day in Braga started with a 6:00 AM breakfast at the hotel. We then made our way to the staging area Joseph was setting up. It was about a 15-minute drive south of the hotel, near a Delphi Automotive plant. It seems the businessman had brought his daughter with him to Europe while he visited different cities to look at buildings where he might start up a company. Karen was 24 years old and supposedly was used to getting her way on most things. Up to the point of being taken, this trip had been one of those times where she had been getting her way.

A few days ago, she and her father, Rick, had been making their way from Lisbon to Braga, stopping in Ponte de Sor and other cities to look at some old manufacturing plants. They had met with several property owners along the way. Their driver was from a tour company and had obviously seen everywhere Rick and Karen had gone and what they were doing. He and the touring company would be one of the first places we'd check out.

So far, the only other place we know they'd stayed was at the Hotel Lago Montargil & Villas. We were getting a picture of their travels, which would give us a chance to look into who they had been in contact with along the way. They had gone from Ponte de Sor and made a stop in Abrantes, looking at some empty buildings. The next day, they'd made a stop in Porto, before getting to Braga, where Karen had been kidnapped. Now that we'd gotten a better picture of where all they'd been, we needed to set up a meeting with Rick and start filling in some gaps in the information we had.

The meeting with Rick was set up for noon at a local restaurant. The initial meeting would be with only Janine and I. John would be at a nearby table in the restaurant, listening to the discussion and keeping an eye out for anyone who might be interested in our meeting with Rick. We only had a couple hours to get to the restaurant and get things set up. That was plenty of time, but we still needed to get started.

Chapter 3

As is normal for me, I sat with my back to the wall in the corner of the restaurant, facing the entrance. John had taken up his position in the other corner, also facing the door. Janine was sitting with me as we waited for Rick. A couple minutes before noon, Rick walked in. As he looked around for who he was supposed to be meeting, Janine started making her way to him. About the time she got a few feet away, another person walked in the door that set off my spidey senses. Janine must have the same spidey sense since she walked past Rick when she saw the guy.

When John saw Janine pass Rick after seeing the guy who walked in, he made his move. He walked toward Rick and the other guy. When he got next to the stranger, he "bumped" into him, giving him a shot that would cause him to pass out in about 10 seconds. As he was apologizing for bumping into him, the stranger started to wobble, which gave John an excuse to grab him by the arm and get him seated in a nearby booth. Everything looked normal enough that no one really paid attention to what was going on.

John got the stranger seated just before he passed out. As they sat there, John managed to get the stranger's wallet. John found his ID and saw that he was from Montargil, Portugal, where Rick and Karen had stayed a couple nights ago. Don't think it's a coincidence that someone from Montargil would be in Braga and come into the same restaurant that Rick came in. This guy was obviously following Rick.

Now that our unwelcome guest had been taken care of, Janine walked back to Rick and guided him to our table. After we introduced ourselves, as Jeremy and Samantha, we started asking Rick about what had happened during his time in Portugal.

He and Karen had flown into Lisbon about a week ago and had spent some time relaxing there. It seems they had been in Europe for a couple weeks, traveling around looking at different buildings where Rick might be able to start a new manufacturing operation. They had been in Nuremberg, Germany the week before, and Karen had gotten sick. They already had plans to travel to Portugal, so they went ahead and came to Lisbon and let Karen get over whatever it was that made her sick. They had gone to a clinic in Lisbon to get some medicines for her, which seemed to help.

While Karen rested and recovered by the pool at the hotel, Rick had worked on getting their arrangements changed for their time in Portugal. He told us that he had to get a different company to drive them around since the one he had originally booked couldn't adjust their driver's schedule. Rick wasn't very happy about it, since he couldn't check out the new company or the driver, but he didn't have much choice.

So, a few days ago, he and Karen left Lisbon, stopping in Montargil, at the hotel we already knew about. Rick said that on the way, he and Karen were talking about their trip so far and where they'd been and the buildings they had seen. Rick said he somewhat noticed the driver listening to them but he really didn't seem to think anything about it since it was somewhat of an uneventful drive from Lisbon to Montargil.

When they got to Montargil, Karen still wasn't feeling 100%, so they got a quick, early dinner and went out to sit by the pool for the evening. Rick said he didn't know what the driver did that afternoon and evening. The next morning, they made their way to Ponte de Sor. Rick said he again noticed the driver listening to their conversation, but still didn't think much about it, even though the drive from Montargil to Ponte de Sor was a little more scenic and should have been more interesting to the driver.

In Ponte de Sor, they looked at a building that had once been used by an American company called Delphi Electronics and Safety to build electronics and steering wheels for cars. The electronics area was in the south part of the building and was a little cleaner than the north part, where the steering wheels were made. Rick said he and Karen spent about 4 hours in the building, checking it out thoroughly.

When they were done, Rick decided to head back to Montargil to spend the night instead of making their way north to Abrantes. It would be easy to get to Abrantes the next morning, leaving from Montargil early. Rick said he really didn't pay much attention to the driver on the way back to Montargil that afternoon. He and Karen were too busy talking about what they had seen in the building. He said it is what they normally do after they visited a site. Karen was very interested in what was going on, which was in contrast to what we'd been told about her being a young lady who always got her way.

Chapter 4

Rick told us that they got up early and had breakfast at the hotel's restaurant. The driver met them as soon as they walked out of the hotel. Rick said the driver seemed a little more "chipper" than the previous days, but again, didn't think too much about it at the time.

They had gotten to Abrantes at about 9 and looked at two buildings there, spending about 3 hours in each one, with lunch in between. Then they started the drive to Porto.

It took a little over 2 hours to get there because of traffic, so they had plenty of time to talk about the Abrantes buildings and the Ponte de Sor building. Rick said he didn't pay much attention to the driver since he and Karen were having a good conversation about what they'd seen and how each building might be able to work for them. He said they also talked about how much each building would cost and how that fit into their business plans.

Rick told us that, looking back, they probably shouldn't have been talking so openly about the money aspect of what they were doing and how much they were willing to spend on the buildings. We agreed it probably wasn't a good idea, but it was too late now to worry about.

He said they got to Porto about 6:30 that evening and got checked into their hotel. They got cleaned up and went out to eat. He said they didn't talk much about the buildings, more about just how the trip had been going. It was a short ride from the hotel to the restaurant, so they ended up getting back to the hotel about 10:00.

The next morning, after breakfast, the driver was again waiting for them at the hotel entrance. They were able to look at three buildings in Porto. Rick said they only spent a couple hours in each since they didn't really seem to be big enough for what they wanted to do. After they finished looking at the third building, they headed to Braga and, interestingly enough, checked into the same hotel where we were staying. Again, looking back, Rick said it was interesting that the driver suggested they walk to the Esperanca Verde for dinner. Janine (Samantha) and I looked at each other, noting the irony of us following the same path Rick and Karen had taken our first night here. On the way back from dinner, Rick said he noticed a group of guys about a block behind them and started to be concerned. He said he probably should have been looking ahead instead, because that's where another group of guys was standing.

Rick said when he turned around from looking at the group following them, the group in front of them jumped out and grabbed him, put a bag over his head and pushed him down to the ground. He said he tried to reach for Karen but they had already taken her. He said he heard tires squealing as a vehicle sped off toward the city.

About that time, the group that had been following him got there and helped him up and got the bag off his head. They told him they had seen everything and got a description of the car that the girl was taken in. Rick said it sounded like the same car they'd been in the past few days from Lisbon to Braga, but that was a common car in Portugal. He said he called the police, even though one of the guys from the group had already called and the police were already on their way. About 5 minutes later, about half a dozen police cars pulled up.

They were at first a little leery about the group of guys around him, but Rick told the police that they had helped him and gotten a description of the car that was used. After a couple minutes, the police were talking to the group of guys, getting as much information from them as possible.

He told us that a couple detectives started asking him questions about what had happened. He said he told them everything about the evening. He then told them he needed to make some calls to the US to try and get some help lined up. Little did they know he was calling the White House in Washington, DC, to get help from the Vice President of the United States.

Rick said the Vice President told him help would be on the way. That it would be impossible for the US government to get involved, but he knew of an organization that was willing and able to help. That was how Janine, John and I got here. It would be nice to be able to thank the Vice President for the recommendation, but we'll never get that chance. We don't let others know who we really are. Even with Rick, he'll only ever know us as Jeremy and Samantha. I'll have to come up with a pseudonym for John, though. I don't want him to feel left out. In this case, I'll just call him Bryce.

We now had a description of the car, even though it was like hundreds of others in Braga. We also know, with help from the group that was following Rick, that there were 4 guys involved in taking Karen. The group was also able to give a little detail about those 4 guys, such as approximate height and weight. That was about all the help they could give since the bad guys were wearing hoodies. Now it was time for Janine, John and me to get to work.

Chapter 5

After Rick left, John and I sat with our "guest" from Montargil. There are two good things about the drug we gave him to knock him out. First, it allows us to give him suggestions on what happened to him. It will be what he remembers happened, even though it is far from being what actually happened. Second, it numbs his skin, which will allow us to insert a GPS tracker without him being aware of it.

Inserting the tracker only took a few seconds. Once it was inserted, we checked to make sure there was a good signal. Now we had to come up with a good story to put in his memory. That didn't take long either. When he wakes up, he'll think he watched Rick come in, sit down and eat lunch. He'll think he also had lunch, so we ended up getting some plates, silverware and glasses to add to his experience. We also cloned his cell phone so we could listen in on his phone calls. Now we'd know if this kidnapping was for a ransom or if it was something worse, like sex trafficking.

Since it had only been a day and a half since Karen was taken, we were hoping Rick would be getting a call soon. When we got his table all set up and had given him his story, John gave him the antidote to the drug. It would take a few minutes for him to come to. That would give us time to get away without him seeing us. John would stay at his table across the room from our guest to make sure everything went as planned. Sure enough, about two minutes later, he opened his eyes. It took him a few more seconds to fully come to and start looking around. After a few shakes of his head, he looked at the plate in front of him, grabbed his napkin, wiped his mouth as if he'd just eaten, and left the restaurant.

He looked both ways to see if he could find Rick, who was long gone by now. However, our Rick lookalike was only a block down the street and getting into a taxi. As lookalike Rick pulled away, our guest hailed a taxi. It took a while for a taxi to get there, which was part of our plan as well, so by the time he got into one, lookalike Rick was also long gone. By the time he got to Rick's hotel to check on whether Rick was there, the real Rick would have been there for about a half hour.

On the way to Rick's hotel, our bad guy made a call to one of his cohorts. He told his buddy that he tracked Rick to the restaurant and watched him eat lunch. He said he also ate lunch so he wouldn't stand out. After the restaurant, he told his buddy that Rick grabbed a taxi and went to his hotel. They talked about getting together in an hour to figure out what to do next.

We now knew when and where they were going to meet. Hopefully, Karen would be there, too, and this whole ordeal would be over. I had John send a couple of his guys to the meeting place to set up surveillance. It turns out the building was an apartment building, so knowing which apartment they were using would have to wait until the guy showed up and we could track him. Fortunately, all the apartments faced the street so John's guys could get a laser mic set up in the building across the street and be ready to go as soon as we found out which apartment they were in.

John's guys had just gotten the laser mic set up when our guest showed up and went into the apartment building. Our tracker was working and let John's guys know that he was in the in the third apartment to the right, on the third floor. The laser mic was pointed to the window and we soon heard their conversation.

It turns out that these two were only a couple worker bees. Definitely not the masterminds of the operation. That is, they weren't the sharpest tools in the shed. They talked a lot about what they'd done and how much trouble they might be in. They also talked about a guy named Piedro Silva, who seemed to be their boss. The question was, was he the boss where they normally worked or the head of the kidnapping operation?

Janine took the name and started running it through the system. It only took a few minutes to get the results. It turns out that Piedro Silva had a criminal record. He had been arrested a couple times for robberies and attempted kidnapping. He must be connected somehow since he'd never been convicted of anything. That's something else Janine will be able to find out.

Janine also found out that Silva was from Lisbon, not Braga. We may have to move our operation to Lisbon. In the meantime, a couple of John's guys headed to Lisbon to find our where Silva was and keep an eye on him. If this was a ransom kidnapping, they could be keeping Karen anywhere between Braga and Lisbon. If it was sex trafficking, they would be more likely to keep her in a more remote location like Montargil or Ponte de Sor. Since Montargil was closer to Lisbon, keeping her there would be more likely.

Chapter 6

About the time Janine was getting information on whether Silva had connections or not, we got a call from Rick. He had just gotten a call from the kidnappers, demanding $3 million ransom. They gave him 24 hours to get the money together and said they'd call him back then with instructions. Fortunately, one of the other things we'd set up was a monitor of Rick's cell phone. It turns out the person who called him was in Braga.

It was a relief for us to know that this was a ransom kidnapping. While not a good thing, it was a lot better than a sex trafficking kidnapping. The results of sex trafficking kidnappings usually never turn out well. That's likely what happened several years ago in Aruba. When the kidnapped person never shows up, alive or dead, it is most likely that they were taken somewhere to be used as a sex slave and, when they've served their purpose, they are disposed of in a way that they will never be found, usually cremated.

We had also cloned Rick's phone and had recorded his conversation with the kidnapper. Janine let us know that Silva was indeed connected. It turns out his brother was a member of the Portuguese Parliament, who also had a history of some nefarious activities. I had John let his guys who were on their way to Lisbon know about Silva's brother and to have them keep an eye on him as well. I asked Janine to get a voice recording of Silva to be able to compare to the recording of the guy who contacted Rick. Even though that voice had been electronically modified, it wouldn't keep Janine from making a comparison. It only took about 20 minutes to get the voice recording of Silva. Janine had used that time to remove the modification from the voice we had recorded. When she got the Silva recording, it only took her a few minutes to let us know it wasn't Silva's voice. It could be that Silva was actually learning something.

He had someone else make the call to keep him out of it. The guys in the apartment, however, evidently never learned anything. They kept talking about what had happened when they helped kidnap Karen. They talked about how the driver Rick and Karen had used contacted Silva about a rich American and his daughter. They said they were contacted by a guy in Braga named Antonio Vargas. Vargas had contracted them to do a job. They didn't know the job was a kidnapping until the night they actually took Karen.

Now it was time for Janine to find out about Vargas. That took a little longer than it did with Silva. It turned out that Vargas had never been arrested. He had been a person of interest in a couple cases, but was never charged. Getting a sample of his voice might be a bit more difficult. But if anyone could do it, it would be Janine.

It's amazing what can happen with the right resources. After about a half hour, Janine finally got a sample of Vargas's voice. It was from a surveillance camera at a restaurant Vargas frequents. How they found out what restaurant he goes to, then managed to get a copy of the video recording of him, is beyond me. I'm just glad our guys back home are on our side! After Janine got that recording, she easily compared it to the voice on Rick's phone. It was a match! Now we have to find Vargas.

That didn't take Janine long, either. You might think when you block your phone number, there's no way anyone can get it. Again, I'm glad our tech guys are on our side! We now had Vargas's cell phone number and could access his GPS. Right now, Vargas was in Braga, not far from a park on the north side of town. It's the same park I'd been to another time I was here. It seems there's a place in the park, on a small hill, where all your visual senses tell you you're going uphill, when, in reality, you're going downhill. But I digress.

We found out that Vargas was in a large house about a hundred meters to the east of the park. It was a little odd that he has such a large house since he wasn't particularly wealthy and didn't have a family. My spidey sense was tingling a little. This may be a combination of ransom kidnapping and a sex trafficking ring. Our first task was to get Karen back, then we'd look into the sex trafficking.

Chapter 7

John got a group of his guys to surveille the house. We needed to know whether Vargas was there and who all came and went. About an hour after the guys were in place, they saw Vargas leave with a couple women. The women were dressed up like they were going to a party. It looked like the women were in their early twenties. John had one of his guys follow the car to see where the party was and who all was attending. My spidey sense told me they were going to be the main attraction at the party and it wasn't going to be much of a party for them.

My heart sank when I realized there was nothing we could do to help them right now. If Karen was being held in the house, we couldn't risk doing anything to help them. We had to get as much information about what was going on and who was involved so we could shut down this ring forever!

About a half hour later, we got the call from John's guy who was tailing Vargas that he'd stopped at a house on the east side of Braga. He'd dropped off the two women and was on his way back. He also said there were no other cars at the house. Even though it was a risk, I asked John to send an extraction team to the house to rescue the two women. They would need to make it look like a home invasion gone bad, where the homeowner was "accidentally" killed. They would tell the women to leave and make them think they were just bystanders in the break-in, not the ones who we were there to set free.

John's team was at the second house in a matter of minutes, once again amazing me with how fast they could get ready. It may just be that since John and I have been working together for so long, he's starting to know what I'm thinking and planned ahead, just in case. Whatever the reason, I'm just glad we were able to free those two women tonight and didn't alarm Vargas. Now we had to find Karen.

We knew we had about a half hour to get some listening devices in place in Vargas's house. It took us about 20 minutes to do that. We also managed to get some cameras put on some of the windows. Now we could see and hear what was going on in there. All the time we were installing the cameras and mics, we made sure no one in the house saw us. Unfortunately, we didn't see any other women in the house. It was hard to tell if there was a basement, but that is the normal place where these kinds of guys keep their victims. I'd have Janine access the building record to see if this house had a basement.

A few minutes later, Vargas returned and went back into the house. We could pretty much see everywhere on the first floor of the house and could hear everything happening on the first and second floors. We just couldn't tell if there was a basement. We saw Vargas walking around the house and talking on the phone. Janine managed to pick up his call and clone his phone. Now we could listen to all of his calls. At this particular time, he was talking about setting up another "party". This time, the "host" was looking for 6 women, who would all need to be in their early 20s. Vargas told him that it wouldn't be a problem. That party was being set up for two days from now. We needed to find Karen quickly so we could start working on taking apart this sex trafficking ring.

Back at the second house, where the first "host" was taken out, John's guy got the host's phone and found Vargas's number. In his best Braga Police Officer voice, he called Vargas and told him that he'd found his number in the victim's phone and that he and Vargas had several phone calls recorded. He let Vargas know that his friend had been found murdered in his home and if he had any information that might help them find out who killed him, even though right now, it looked more like a home invasion gone wrong. True to form for a sex trafficker, Vargas only said he had been doing some business with the guy over the past several weeks. He obviously didn't ask about the two girls. He probably didn't even care. He'd just write them off as a business loss. Sickening!

After the call from the "police officer", Vargas made a call to Silva. That confirmed the connection to Silva! Now we need to find the rest of Silva's crew. And now we have Silva's phone number. That will make it a lot easier to keep track of him and find more of his crew. Janine sent the information to the team in Lisbon that was tracking Silva. But getting Silva was our second task. Our first one is finding and rescuing Karen.

Janine finally got a copy of the plans for Vargas's house. It did have a basement. We had about 12 hours left before the 24-hour deadline was up. That would give us time to track down a number of Silva's other lieutenants, which was something Headquarters would be doing while we were breaching Vargas's house. The women Vargas was keeping had to be in the basement. That's most likely where Karen was as well.

John got some of his extraction team members to Vargas's house. The plan would be to wait until Vargas had been off his phone for a while and went upstairs, then we would set up a cell phone jammer. We'd had a chance to get a good idea of the layout of the house from our surveillance and from the floorplans Janine had obtained. We had also looked for and identified all of the security devices in the house. It would be easy for John's guys to disable all of them at one time, right before they breached the house.

The plan would be to turn on the cell phone jammer, disable the security system, and enter the house quietly. One team would go upstairs and get Vargas, hopefully alive, and to secure the second floor. A second team would secure the first floor. The third team would carefully make their way down to the basement. There may still be booby traps set up. This team was the best at detecting and disarming IEDs!

After checking the door to the basement for any wires, they slowly opened it. There were no lights on, so they turned on their night-vision equipment. This would also help them detect any trip wires since the infrared lighting they used would "illuminate" the wires. They used mirrors on long poles to check under each step for pressure plates that might set off an IED. On the third step from the bottom, they found something that looked interesting. They could see wiring leading up to a switch at the top of the stairs.

Flipping the switch would turn off the sensor. It was likely left on to prevent any of the women from getting very far if they managed to get out of where they were being held. In any case, the team would skip the third step. Better safe than sorry. After the stairs were secured, the team made their way to the basement. There was a small area there, with about a dozen doors. The team checked each door for wires. None of them were wired. They found a key rack on the wall at the bottom of the stairs. There was a numbered key for each numbered door. The team was very quiet, so they could hear women's voices behind each door as they checked it for wires. Except for door number 8. There was no talking there, only the sounds of footsteps pacing back and forth.

That was likely where Karen was being held. Using the key for door 8, we slowly opened the door. We opened it slowly anticipating that if it was Karen, she would have found a way to attack Vargas when he opened it. As soon as the door was opened a crack, a chair leg came crashing through. Yep, that was probably Karen.

We quickly let her know we were there to rescue her. She wasn't fully convinced until we got into the room and she saw the team's uniforms and knew it wasn't Vargas. When we finally got the door fully opened and had the lights on, we confirmed that it was, indeed, Karen. The team quickly led her up to the first floor where Janine (Samantha) was waiting. Janine took her out of the house, escorted by the first-floor extraction team members, and to a safehouse we'd set up, to give her a chance to get cleaned up and put on clean clothes before we took her to see Rick.

Chapter 8

While the basement team was rescuing Karen, the second-floor team was getting Vargas. He put up very little resistance. While I wouldn't have minded if he had put up a lot and managed to get himself killed in the process, he was much more useful to us alive. He would help us find Silva and the rest of Silva's ring, whether he wanted to or not.

After about 30 minutes of letting Vargas know that we weren't police and didn't have to follow police rules, he finally realized the situation he was in. He started singing like a bird after a we suggested some of the techniques we'd start using if he didn't start talking. While we seldom actually used any of them, the idea of having some of those things done were enough to motivate the suspect to help us. This was no exception.

Vargas told us he would have to call Silva in about an hour to report in and give him an update on what happened to the guy in the second house and the two women who had been taken there. We turned off the cell phone jammer to see if Vargas had missed any calls, especially any from Silva. Fortunately, he hadn't. That meant our extraction had been completely successful. Karen would soon be back with her father and Vargas would be taken into custody with all his body parts still attached.

Back in the basement, after Karen had been taken away, the rest of the doors were opened. In ten of the rooms, there were about 6 women each. The nightmares for 60 young women came to an end tonight, 58 here and the 2 from the second house! One of the doors that was opened was evidently used as a dressing room. There was a shower and a closet full of fancy clothes. We had anticipated finding several women, but 60 was way more than we imagined.

We only brought a couple dozen sets of new clothing, so we sent two of our female agents to get more new clothes. In the meantime, we let all of the women take showers and get cleaned up as best they could. We found some women's clothing in the closets on the second floor that could be used. With those clothes and what we brought, about 40 women managed to get cleaned up and ready to be transported to a second safehouse we had set up.

About the time the first group of women were ready to go to the safehouse, the rest of the clothing arrived. It was too bad we had to keep them here to let them get cleaned up, but it was bittersweet that they used the house they had used to get ready to go to their "parties" to now get ready to start their journeys home. Only this time, it was in the showers and bedrooms in the more luxurious parts of the house.

After a couple hours, all 58 women had managed to take showers and get into new clothes. The female agents escorted the last 18 women to the second safehouse. This part of the job was done. We rescued Karen and shut down this particular house. Now Janine and I were able to reunite Karen with Rick. That is always a good feeling. I called Rick and let him know that Samantha and I were on our way to his hotel. I didn't tell him anything else.

Janine and I went to the safehouse where Karen was staying. I introduced Janine and I to her as Samantha and Jeremy. We told her that we were going to take her to her father. You could see her eyes brighten and tears starting to well up. That was another great thing about this part of the job. Seeing the pure joy in the faces of those we've helped. It doesn't happen very often in our line of work, but when it does, it's a great feeling.

It took us about 10 minutes to get from the safehouse to Rick's hotel. The streets were pretty empty at this time of the morning. We got Karen out of the car and were halfway up to the hotel door when Rick came running out and Karen ran toward her dad. Janine and I took a glance at each other and each of us had a tear running down our cheeks. We let Rick and Karen have some time together. When they finished their embrace, they turned to us and gave us each a hug. It was a great end to the first part of this mission. Now back to work.

Chapter 9

John had been with Vargas when he reported in with Silva. Vargas had told Silva that it looked like it had been a burglar who just happened to break into the guy's house and killed their client. Silva asked about the two women who had been there. Vargas told Silva that the police hadn't said anything about them, so he assumed they managed to get away. He told Silva that he would go to the neighborhood after sunrise to see if he could find them.

Little did either of them know that, after we secured Vargas's house, we picked up those two women and taken them to the second safehouse with the others who were rescued.

We had coached Vargas to encourage Silva to check on the other houses to make sure everything was okay. He told Silva that he was a little concerned about the coincidence of the burglar happening to be there the night he'd taken the two women there. Silva agreed, even though he also agreed that it was highly unlikely anything was going to happen at the other houses. It seems our plan was executed flawlessly. With John and his team, that was the way it normally happened.

After Vargas finished talking to Silva, John's guys took him to the holding room in the staging area Joseph had set up. One of John's guys stayed at Vargas's house with his cell phone in case Silva was able to track it. The rest of John's guys had gotten to the staging area by then. They kept their faces covered until Vargas had been securely locked in the holding room. About twenty minutes after they had locked Vargas up, Janine and I got there. We could see the various emotions on the faces of John's guys. They were happy they managed to safely rescue Karen and the 60 other women, but you could also see the disgust in their faces that this kind of thing goes on. It's good to have those kinds of people on our team.

Since we'd all been up nearly 24 hours, we decided we all needed some rest. The team in Lisbon would be monitoring Silva's phone. After about two hours, Silva started making calls. Our team in Lisbon was able to track all of the calls and the locations of each person Silva called. It turned out that there were seven other houses. Four of them were in different areas in Lisbon, two were in Porto and one was in Abrantes. After Silva called all of his lieutenants, he called Vargas's number. Our guy at Vargas's house, who sounded a lot like Vargas, answered. Silva told him he'd called all the other houses and asked Vargas why he hadn't left to try and find the women from last night. Good thing we'd left Vargas's phone at his house since it was now obvious that he could track it.

Our guy told Silva he was just heading out the door to do just that. He said he'd gotten sick on something he'd eaten last night and had been throwing up for the past couple hours. He told Silva that all he had now was a sore throat, so he'd be in the area where their client was killed and the women were missing in about 45 minutes. Silva told him he hoped he felt better and to let him know ASAP what he found out.

That would give us some time to get guys deployed to the seven other houses. Joseph woke us up to let us know what had happened with Silva. Three hours sleep was better than none, I guess. Joseph had already sent teams to the seven houses. Since we were closest to the ones in Porto, Janine and I headed to one of them and John headed to the other one. We managed to get a couple helicopters to take some of John's guys to Abrantes and Lisbon. We already had some additional resources in the Lisbon area, so, along with John's guys already there, we'd have plenty of resources to carry out the mission.

We had to coordinate our extractions to the second. We couldn't afford to let one lieutenant warn Silva. The plan would be very similar to what we'd just done at Vargas's house. Since it was mid-morning now, we'd likely have until about seven, since most of the "parties" started around eight.

The phones of all the lieutenants were being monitored. The good thing was, it was Sunday, so there probably were few, if any, parties planned for tonight. Most of the clients actually had day jobs so having a party on Sunday night wouldn't be likely.

The Lisbon team had sent us all the phone numbers of the lieutenants, so we were able to monitor their calls and locations. Right now, all of them were at their houses. Even Silva was at his house. Since his brother was in the Parliament, taking him would be a little more difficult. And since he was the head of this particular sex trafficking ring, it was likely he'd have a security force protecting him. We're just not sure how many would be on that protection detail. The most experienced extraction team would be sent to Silva's house, with orders to take out Silva's security detail. If they could take Silva alive, they were to try.

But just like Seal Team 6, who were tasked to take Bin Laden in Pakistan alive if possible, if that didn't happen, no one would have a problem. Based on all our intel, Silva was the ultimate leader of this particular sex trafficking ring. Taking him out would prevent him from starting another ring in the future. And if he were dead, his MP brother wouldn't be able to get him out of being arrested.

With all that in mind, I decided to wait until three in the morning to execute our plan. That would give our guys a little more time to get into place and to get a little more rest. I asked John to have one guy set up at each house to monitor what was going on.

By midnight, all the teams were in place at each lieutenant's house and at Silva's house. We started our time synchronization at 12:30. All of the teams needed to act at one time. Based on our takedown of the neo-Nazi groups in Germany a while ago, acting as one was built into these guys' DNA. Now came the hard part. Waiting. Not something we liked to do. At our 1:00 AM check, all teams reported that all lieutenants and Silva were at their respective houses. The team at Silva's house reported that there were only three security guys on site. Since we had six guys at his house, taking out the security guys and Silva shouldn't be difficult. But we are never complacent. We always expect things will not always go as planned. With our training and experience, handling those unexpected situations didn't require a lot of thought, just reaction.

At the 2:30 AM check, all of our teams reported that they were ready. They all had managed to get cameras and listening devices in place without being detected. There would only be one more check-in before we initiated our plan. Just like at Vargas's house, at exactly 3:00, the cell jammers would be turned on, the security systems would be deactivated, the teams would enter the houses and every bad guy would be eliminated. Since all of our guys would have silencers, we wouldn't be waking up the neighbors, so the local police wouldn't be called. The greatest risk, obviously, would be at Silva's house. The security guys there probably had some level of training. Nothing nearly as good as our guys, but they would probably have guns.

The Silva house team would have the most difficulty, which is why we sent the best team there. It was getting really close to H-Hour. At 2:55, we made our final synchronization check. Making sure 7 teams were coordinated to the second was a difficult task. The body cameras on each team member were turned on and checked for the last time. All of them showed exactly the same time, to the nearest tenth of a second. From now on, there wouldn't be any more communications until after all houses were secured.

30

Chapter 10

At exactly 3:00, the team Janine and I were with executed the plan. In 1 minute, all team members were in the house and the lieutenant in that house was in no longer a threat. The team then found the door to the basement. The same process of checking the door for IEDs was followed. When none were found, the stairs were checked for IEDs as well. Just as in Vargas's house, the third step from the bottom had a pressure sensor connected to a switch at the top of the stairs.

Once in the basement, we found four doors. The keys were all on a keyring next to the first door. Each door was checked, just like at Vargas's house. Fortunately, no IEDs were found on any of them. We started with door number one. We obviously startled the women in the room. When they saw we weren't the lieutenant, they started calming down. The commotion in this room got the women in the other rooms startled. We started opening the other rooms, letting one of the women from the first room be the first to go in. When all the rooms had been opened, there ended up being 12 women. Four each from three rooms and the fourth room being a shower/dressing room.

When we made sure we had all the women who had been kept here, we led them out of the basement and out to a waiting bus to transport them to the Porto safehouse. We made sure we had plenty of clean clothes this time. The safehouse also had four bathrooms and six rooms to use to get dressed and finish getting ready to go home.

Our team was the second team to get to the safehouse. The other Porto team had gotten there about 2 minutes before us. There were 9 women from the second house in Porto. While the first group were showering and getting dressed, the women from the second house were getting something to eat and drink. They all looked like they hadn't eaten well for quite a while. When the first few women from the second house made their way into the kitchen/dining area, there were looks of recognition. After a second or so, two of the women ran toward each other and hugged. It turns out they were sisters who had been abducted a couple months ago. Each had been told that the other was dead. It was how they had been more easily controlled.

Now that the two Porto houses had been secured and the women now in the safehouse, we made our way back to Braga and the staging area. We got there a lot quicker with the helicopter had available to us. On the way to Braga, we started getting updates on the other five houses. All of them had been safely entered, the lieutenant taken out, and the women rescued and taken to their respective safehouses. All the women were taking showers, getting cleaned up and being fed. Seven houses, seven successful extractions. It was a great morning. Now we just needed to hear from the team at Silva's house.

We got to Braga and made our way to the staging area. As we walked in the door, Joseph had a concerned look on his face. The mission at Silva's house was somewhat of a success. The team had successfully entered the house and taken out four security guys before they could fire a shot. They had made their way to Silva's room, waking him up. When Silva went for a gun, the team fired a shot to his forehead. That part of the mission went off without a hitch.

When the team split up to search the rest of the house, one of the team members walked into a room where two other security guys had been sleeping. They had heard the team moving through the house and were waiting for them to enter their room. As soon as the door opened, they shot our guy. As soon as they fired, the rest of the team made their way to the room and took out the security guys, with a vengeance. We were still waiting to hear how our guy was. While we were waiting, we started going through the camera feeds from the team in Silva's house, particularly the feed from the guy who was shot. We needed to figure out what went wrong. As we watched the video, getting just past the point where he was shot, we got a report from the team leader at Silva's house. Our guy had taken a bullet to his chest, but his vest stopped it. It just knocked him out. He had also been shot in his left arm, which was now being taken care of. The sigh of relief could be heard all over the room!

Chapter 11

Now there were 60 women from Braga, 21 from Porto, 8 from Abrantes, and 120 from the four locations in Lisbon who were going home. As we thought about it, we again were overwhelmed with a feeling of satisfaction. In less than 24 hours, we had eliminated a sex trafficking ring (with only Vargas still alive), and freed 209 women from a horrendous captivity. This may have been the only sex trafficking ring in Portugal. However, it's not the only sex trafficking ring in existence.

It wasn't going to be us, but the results of this mission were going to be made very public. We'd make sure it was well known that the people who took down this ring would be coming after other sex traffickers around the world, and that what happened to the guys in this ring would be happening to them. Soon. They would know that the leader and all of his lieutenants had been killed.

Vargas wasn't killed in the mission. He was questioned about whether he knew of any other rings in Portugal. According to him, there weren't. He was also asked if he knew others like Silva in other countries. He said he'd heard about a guy named Antonio Garza in Malaga, Spain, and another guy in Madrid named Marco Martinez. He wasn't sure if they were the leaders of their rings or just guys like him, running houses. I made sure our organization sent teams to those cities to check those guys out. Based on our success in Portugal, they would be very successful in Spain.

After we felt we had all the information we needed from Vargas, we strapped him down in a chair, with a bag over his head. He sat there for a couple hours, anticipating what was going to happen to him next. Every few minutes, someone would come into the room and appear to chamber a round in a pistol. It's a very distinctive sound. The pistol would be empty. After about a minute or so, the guy would put the pistol up to Vargas's head and pull the trigger. There would be the typical click when the hammer falls. With the click, Vargas would jump. This was done several times. Each time, Vargas was told that the feeling he had when the trigger was pulled was only a fraction of what the 60 women had felt while he opened the doors to their rooms.

After a couple hours of this treatment, with 60 gun clicks, the bag was taken off. When he opened his eyes, the 60 women he'd held captive were standing in front of him.

You could see the fear in his face. Now he was going to be the one who was tormented and degraded. One by one, each woman went up to Vargas and slapped him, then spit on him. Each woman was given the opportunity to go up to him again and say whatever they wanted to say to him, or to slap him again. All 60 women proved their strength by walking up to him, whispering something to him, then slapping him again.

When all 60 women had finished with Vargas, you could see the confidence in their faces. They had been held captive by this evil man, but they survived. Now, they had seen their tormentor for what he was, a coward.

Chapter 12

Most of the time, when we'd captured or killed the bad guys, the mission would be over. Not this time. We still had a few loose ends to wrap up. First, we made a visit to Rick and Karen to make sure they were getting along.

Once again, as we met them in the lobby of the hotel, both Rick and Karen gave both Janine and I hugs. Our agency was going to provide them with a security detail for the rest of their trip. When it's requested by the Vice President of the United States, it gets done. I asked Rick to thank the Vice President for trusting us to get his daughter back. Of course, Rick said he would, not knowing that when he told the VP that Jeremy and Samantha got his daughter back, the VP would never know who we were, even if he asked our Director who Jeremy and Samantha were. Even our Director didn't know we'd used those aliases.

Now that the happy part of our mission was completed, we got back to finishing up our task of cleaning up the rest of those involved in this horrific ordeal. With the phones of all the lieutenants and records we'd found at each of the houses, we were able to find out who all the clients had been. They are just as much to blame for all of this as the lieutenants were. If there were no clients, there would be no need for the sex trafficking rings. It was time to make sure there would be no more demand for this kind of thing for a long time. We knew it may only be a temporary fix, but it would definitely send a message to clients all over the world.

Not only would we be coming after the sex trafficking ring leaders, but their clients as well.

The first group would be those from Vargas's house. His client list was very long. Fortunately, one on his list had already been taken care of. Now for the rest. Some might think that we had no right to be judge, jury and executioner. They may have a point, but the women who were victimized never got a chance to have a judge and jury before they were held in captivity. They didn't have a judge or jury sentence them to the parties they had to attend.

In addition to the clients, we also found records of various local officials and police officers who had been paid to look the other way while all of this was going on. They would be the first to be taken out. There's nothing worse than crooked public officials and dirty cops.

Our teams had been able to get a lot of well-deserved rest. Our guy who got shot in Silva's house was healing nicely. He still had a big bruise on his chest, but it was only a bruise, not a hole. His arm had been stitched and was healing as well. All of us were ready to finish this mission, and we all knew what that entailed. The details of who and when were laid out.

Each dirty public official and dirty cop had been identified and their pictures given to the team. Each team member was also given a note to leave on each of their targets. It said, "Essa pessoa sabia sobre o anel de tráfico sexual operando em sua cidade. Eles ajudaram a fazer acontecer ou olharam para o outro lado. Isso é o que acontece com pessoas assim." This translates to "This person knew about the sex trafficking ring operating in your city. They either helped make it happen or looked the other way. This is what happens to people like that."

Our cleanup operation would begin at midnight. There were 17 on the list in Braga. Two of our guys were assigned to each person on the list. This would be another coordinated effort in each city. There were 8 in Porto, 3 in Abrantes and 37 in Lisbon, including Silva's brother, the MP.

Silva's MP brother had four team members assigned to take him out. We made sure our guys knew that collateral damage to family members was not acceptable. Only the people on the list were targets. Of course, any security details that got in the way were fair game.

Precisely at midnight, all teams breached their target's house. Within 10 minutes, all teams had reported success. The only team that reported more than the target being encountered was the team taking out the MP. There were two security people at his house. Two members of that team managed to capture and secure the two security guards while the other two team members eliminated the target.

All teams reported that no family members were harmed and notes were left on each target. By 1:00 AM, all team members had returned to their respective staging areas. If what was reported on the local news the next day didn't put the fear of God in all corrupt officials, I don't know what would. News of what happened in Portugal spread throughout Europe. By the next day, 20 different sex trafficking rings were eliminated by local officials, in 12 different European countries. I suspect more would be eliminated soon. Unfortunately, the ring in Malaga, Spain, was not included in the news report. I gave the team there the green light to take out the leader and all his lieutenants that night. The next morning, the news from Malaga was much like the news out of the Portuguese cities a couple nights ago about the sex trafficking ring.

Our team in Malaga was able to get the same kind of names we had gotten in the Portuguese cities. The corrupt officials and the clients. The next night, at midnight, all the corrupt officials were eliminated. The same message, in Spanish of course, was left on each target. When this was reported the next day, the number of sex trafficking rings in Europe that were eliminated by local officials increased by 30. It was hard to fathom that there were at least 50 sex trafficking rings in Europe. The good news is, there are 52 that have been eliminated. And yes, the one in Madrid was one that was eliminated by locals.

In addition to the 52 rings eliminated, nearly 500 local officials and dirty cops were arrested all over Europe. I'm not sure if their fate is better than the ones in Portugal or not.

Normally crooked public officials and dirty cops don't fare well in prison. When the other inmates find out who they are and that they were allowing sex trafficking rings to go on in their cities, a different kind of sex trafficking happens in the prison. It's usually not a pretty sight for the officials and cops.

Our next task was to eliminate those who created the demand. We'd wait a couple days to let things settle down a little. So far, only the sex rings and corrupt officials had been eliminated. Doing that in Portugal had been very effective in getting the rings and officials taken care of around Europe. We knew there were, unfortunately, more rings in Europe and other places around the world. It was time to put the fear of God in those who created the demand, the clients.

A new note was written in Portuguese that said, "This person was a client of the sex trafficking ring that was recently eliminated in your city. He was one of many who created a need for the sex trafficking ring here. He is one of many tonight who will no longer be around to create that need in the future. Let him be a warning to others who think trafficking women for sex is okay. It is definitely not okay."

After the news reports started dying down about the sex trafficking rings and corrupt public officials, I decided it was time to put our latest plan into motion. There were a lot of guys on our client list. More than we had on our team. Each two-man team was assigned 8 clients who lived near each other. Clients with the most "parties" were highest priority.

Those with only one or two might even be spared, depending on how many higher priority clients we thought we'd be able to take out before morning.

There were still several very low priority clients left when the teams had been given their assignments. Once we'd eliminated the assigned clients, we may come back to the very low priority clients and just go to their houses and give them the scare of their lives. We'd just take their picture and send it, along with their address to the local media, along with a modified note. Since he wasn't eliminated, the third paragraph of the note would say. "Many of the others like him will no longer be around to create that need in the future."

The plan was set in motion at midnight. By 3:00 AM, all the teams had reported that their assignments had been eliminated. Several teams were going to go ahead with the "scare'em" list. By 5:00 AM, all of those clients had been served their notice. By 6:00 AM, all of the teams had returned to the staging area. It had been another successful night. The news reports later that day would let us know just how successful it was.

The news reports were as gruesome as we'd expected. The reports said there were 96 men killed overnight who had taken part in the sex trafficking ring. Another 30 pictures of men had been received and police had been sent to their houses to question them. All 30 had been arrested. All this was just in Braga. The same kinds of reports were coming in from Porto, Abrantes, and Lisbon. By the end of the day, the total number of clients who had been eliminated totaled over 600 and the number arrested was close to 200.

Fortunately, the police were asking any others who had taken part in using women from the sex traffickers to turn themselves in, for their own safety. This part of the mission was having the same effect all over Europe. Another 23 trafficking rings were shut down. Another 70 corrupt officials had been arrested. Nearly 1000 clients had turned themselves in, saying they feared being killed. I'd say we'd had a significant impact.

By the way, I couldn't forget the victims in all of this. With over 70 sex trafficking rings shut down, nearly 1500 women were now free. They were getting ready to finally go home. They wouldn't have the same satisfaction the women from Braga had, of facing their captor and tormenting him. But they would soon be home with their families. And that was the end of a very good mission.

Chapter 13

Janine, John and I got together at a local bar to celebrate and review everything that had happened. Actually, there was more celebrating than reviewing. We could always review the mission. This would be a time to think about what we had done. In less than a week, we had rescued Karen and returned her to her father, we had shut down a sex trafficking ring in Portugal and eliminated everyone in the ring. Oh, and just to tie things up, Vargas hung himself in his cell. Sorry about the pun there. And that was just in Portugal.

All over Europe, sex trafficking rings had been shut down. Nearly 1500 women were on their way home after months, if not years, of being held captive. Dozens of corrupt officials and dirty cops all over Europe had been arrested, along with the leaders of the sex trafficking rings. And hundreds of clients had been arrested and identified as sex offenders. Something that will haunt them for the rest of their miserable lives. Overall, a pretty good job! Maybe too good.

About half way through our third beer, I got a call from our Director. It seems the Vice President was so impressed with what we'd done, he wanted to thank us personally, along with the President of the United States. As I've said before, we don't do things like that. But the Director was very insistent. He wanted the three of us to get to Washington, DC, as soon as possible. John was adamant that he was not going to be there. I convinced the Director to let John stay out of it. We'd get as many of John's guys there as we could. They'd all be able to hide their faces, much the same way they had on missions.

The meeting would take place at Joint Base Andrews and would be part of the President's trip to some other location. There could absolutely be no cameras allowed and Janine and I would be introduced as Samantha and Jeremy. I am assuming Rick and Karen would be there, so we'd have to stick with those identities. I tried to throw up as many obstacles as I could to keep it from happening, but in the end, they agreed to everything, so we were stuck. Two weeks from today, we'd be at Joint Base Andrews, meeting with the President and Vice President of the United States.

So, what to do for two weeks? John said he had really enjoyed his time in Nice, France, but we might not do a lot of the things he did, since we were becoming a "couple". So, Janine and I decided to head back to the US for our R&R. She knew some people near Nashville, Tennessee who might be fun to visit. It's settled. We'll go see Janine's friends Brian and Mary in Mount Juliet, Tennessee.

Janine and Mary had been roommates at Indiana University in Bloomington, Indiana. Mary knew her as Brianna. Now I'm not sure if Janine's real name is Janine or Brianna. I guess it doesn't really matter. After all, I'm not sure if my real name is Larry or Justin or something else. After a while in this business, it's hard to keep track. For now, I'll just be Jeremy and Janine will be Brianna.

Chapter 14

We'd spent about 4 days debriefing before we were able to leave Portugal. After the flight from Lisbon, Janine and I made our way to our hotel. Even though Mount Juliet is only a few miles from the Nashville Airport, and Brian and Mary had invited us to stay with them, we decided it wasn't a good idea. Besides, they weren't expecting us until tomorrow. The JW Marriott Nashville is downtown, so it will be easy to get to experience Downtown Nashville. We could only stay here for 4 nights before we had to go to Washington, DC. Somehow, the Organization managed to get us set up in a room on the 33rd floor, the top floor of the hotel. Since they were paying for it, I didn't complain.

After we got cleaned up, we made our way to Demos' on 3rd Ave for dinner. It wasn't too crowded. After all, it was a Wednesday night. We each had one of their sandwiches. My seven-ounce Cheeseburger was great. Janine had a Mozzarella Cajon Chicken Sandwich, which was also fantastic. It was really good to have an American meal.

After dinner, we went over a block to 2nd Ave. It is a street lined with "Honky Tonks". At the north end was a Hooters and on the south end was a Hard Rock Café. We weren't interested in either of those tonight since we'd already eaten. The Wildhorse Saloon looked promising. The dance floor and stage seemed to be one, not that either of us were good at dancing. We ended up on the second of three floors. It was a little quieter. After a few beers and a lot of country music, we decided to call it a night.

Back at the JW, on the 33rd floor, the city below looked awesome. Across the Cumberland River was the stadium the Titans played in. Just to the north was the State Capitol Building. Next door to the northeast was

Bridgestone Arena and to the east was the Nashville Music City Center. Too bad we weren't going to be able to go to any of those places. At least not this time.

45

Janine and I got up early and took advantage of the Concierge Floor Lounge. There were all kinds of fresh fruits and breakfast dishes. It was hard to not eat too much. For a second, I thought about the women we had rescued and how little they'd been able to eat. But I have trained myself to not think about things like that too long. Yes, it was a very bad situation. Yes, we were able to free hundreds of women who are now home. That mission was a great success, but now it is over and Janine and I can enjoy breakfast together again, alone, for the first time since the morning we left Ko Olina to go zip lining.

After breakfast, we made our way to Brian and Mary's in Mount Juliet. It was nice to be able to spend a few days with "normal" people. But as always, all good things must come to an end. After spending the last three days in Nashville, it was time to head to Washington, DC.

Chapter 15

The flight to Reagan National was the shortest hop I'd been on for a while. We made our way to the Key Bridge Marriott, passing the Pentagon on the way, as well as the entrance to Arlington National Cemetery. Several of my friends were buried there. When I have time, I manage to visit their graves, as well as the Tomb of the Unknowns. It's a sobering thought. When I die, I don't know if I'll have a grave in Arlington or will just be remembered as one of the Unknowns. Kind of a morbid thought as we're getting ready to meet the President and Vice President tomorrow.

We had a package waiting for us when we checked in. It was our credentials to get us onto Joint Base Andrews tomorrow. Headquarters knew I would be going as Jeremy and Janine was going as Samantha, but we hadn't used a last name. HQ had to come up with last names for us. They must have heard we have been getting to know each other better, since they gave us the same last names on our creds. Not very original, either, I might add. We were going as Jeremy and Samantha Jones. I guess Smith might have been even more conspicuous.

According to the documents in the package, we are scheduled to meet the President and Vice President in the PAX Terminal, which is part of Andrews Air Force Base.

While it was only about a forty-minute drive, we needed to be there at least an hour before the President and Vice President. Even though we were the ones invited by the VP, we still had to go through a pretty rigorous security check.

Guess I can't blame them. Our team is made up of some pretty talented people who have been known to kill. Very few people actually know that, but I'm sure the President and Vice President did. As did a few in the Secret Service.

So, taking a little extra time to make sure the Secret Service was satisfied we were OK wouldn't be a problem. We decided to leave even a couple hours earlier than we needed to. It would give us time to make a stop at Arlington National Cemetery. I hadn't been able to visit my buddies there for quite a while. My other set of credentials allowed us to drive through the Cemetery to the site they were buried.

It was a bright, sunny day and the air was clean from a rain shower that had gone through last night. It took about 10 minutes to get to where we needed to go, not far from the Tomb of the Unknowns.

I took Janine to each of the graves and told her about each of the guys buried there. About Robert, who was killed in Iraq, about five feet away from me and likely saved my life. I had carried his body back to our Hum Vee. Then there was James who also died in Iraq when he tripped an IED. He knew he'd tripped it and jumped over it to try to protect the rest of our squad. We had to gather up what was left of him to bring back to the base. He was awarded the Silver Star and Congressional Medal of Honor for saving the rest of us.

Third was Andrew. He was a very special guy. Even though he was the youngest on our team, he ended up quickly fitting right in. He was quick witted and told the best jokes. He would have gone a long way if he hadn't been killed trying to help a young Afghan boy wearing a suicide vest.

Last, but certainly not least, was Michael. We'd always called him Mikey, since he looked a lot like the kid from the old LIFE cereal commercial. It took a lot to stop Mikey.

Our team had been on a mission in the mountains of Afghanistan, northeast of Kabul, not far from the Tajikistan border, near Mastuj. We'd been helo'd in about 3 clicks north of Mastuj, on the far side of the mountain peak. Our intel guys told us there was a shipment of money at the National Bank of Pakistan there that was destined for the Taliban. I didn't tell Janine the whole story since it would take more time than we had left. During that mission, Mikey was shot in his left arm, both legs and finally in the neck. Even with all those wounds, Mikey managed to take out seven Taliban and helped us get the money back to the pickup point. We were just starting to re-dress his wounds when he looked me in the eyes and told me to keep up the good fight. Then he died. He's why I'm doing what I'm doing now. I'm fighting the good fight.

Chapter 16

Janine and I got to the PAX Terminal on JBA with about 15 minutes to spare. The windows where we went were tinted, so we could see out, but no one could see in. About 20 of John's guys were there with their faces covered. One of them looked like it might actually be John, so I went up to him and asked. Yep, it was John. Then Joseph stepped up and said hi. It was a really good feeling to know they were there. They deserved to be recognized, figuratively, by the President and Vice President of the United States.

Marine One was just getting ready to land, bringing the President and Vice President from the White House. Even though these guys were some of the toughest in the world, you could still feel their anticipation. It's amazing how guys who faced some of the worst people in the world without any sense of fear, could be anxious about meeting two people. You could see them straining to see where Marine One was and how soon it would be before the President and VP would make it into the Terminal.

As the rotor noise from Marine One died down, the anxiety built up. Two minutes later, the President, Vice President, First Lady and Second Lady came into the Terminal, followed by Rick, his wife, and Karen. While the team were no longer in the military, they had formed up and saluted when the entourage entered. The President and VP quickly returned the salute and told them to be at-ease.

The group started to head toward Janine and me, but I gave them a quick look toward the team, gesturing that they should great them first. He got the message and went over to them.

Everyone in the entourage personally shook each team members' hand and thanked them individually for what they'd done. After all of the team had been greeted and thanked, the President led the entourage to Janine and I. Before he could say anything, Karen and her mom rushed up to us and gave us big hugs, tears running down their cheeks. Rick was just a little more subdued as he gave me a heart-felt handshake and Janine a hug.

Then the President and First Lady came up to us and shook our hands and thanked us and our team for all our great work. He was definitely well informed, since he thanked us for what we had done in Taiwan and in Germany, as well as what we had just done in Portugal. The First Lady had a little puzzled look on her face since she obviously didn't know about those missions, or any of the other dozens of prior missions. After he thanked us again, calling us Jeremy and Samantha a few times, he left and made his way to a small stage where he'd be making some remarks.

Then the Vice President and his wife came up to us and thanked us again for what we'd done to help his friend, Rick. He told us that he'd been briefed about the existence of our team, but had never expected to need our services and to actually meet us. He called us Jeremy and Samantha a few times as well, once with a wink, acknowledging that those were probably not our real names. After a few minutes of talking about Rick's family, the VP and his wife also made their way to the stage, along with Rick, his wife, and Karen.

The President spoke for about 15 minutes, thanking us once again for all that we'd done to rescue Karen and shut down so many sex trafficking rings in Europe. It wasn't the typical political speech we've all heard before. This was a heart-felt thank you speech to the guys who put their lives on the line to save others. He got into a little of the details of things we already knew about, since we were there, but the First Lady,

Second Lady, Rick, his wife and Karen all had a look of astonishment, and tears, on their faces. The VP just looked on in admiration, since he'd obviously already been briefed on all of this and wasn't as shocked as the others.

The President did tell us a few things we didn't know about. As a result of what we had done in Portugal, the FBI was able to shut down nearly 30 sex trafficking rings in the United States, and other countries around the world were starting to really crack down on sex trafficking in their countries. While it won't stop it everywhere and may not keep more from springing up, the President said he would be announcing to the world that if he found out about more sex trafficking rings, he knew how to get the group, us, there to do to them what they'd done in Portugal.

After a long round of applause, the President's group again walked through the team shaking hands and thanking them. This was a little more casual, like a group of friends at a party. It took about a half hour for the President and his entourage to start making their way to the exit. As he was about to go through the door, he stopped, quickly turned to the team and gave them a salute. The VP quickly followed suit. As one, the team turned to them and returned the salutes. The significance of the President and Vice President of the United States initiating the salute was not wasted on the team. And having them hold their salutes until the team dropped theirs was also very telling of how much the team was respected by the President and Vice President.

When things started calming down, the team members started making their way to where they had come in and get on the bus that would take them to the transport plane that was waiting to take them back to their training base. Even I didn't know where that was. John and Joseph stayed a few minutes to thank us for encouraging the team to make this trip. It was something that had never happened before and likely would never happen again. I told John to thank his team again for what they had done in Portugal and for what they caused to happen around the world. Because of them, the world was definitely a safer place.

Now Janine and would have to decide where we'd go for our R&R. The Irish countryside sounded like a good idea. We'll have to check out to see if it's lucky for us.